How to Overcome Communication Barriers in the Workplace

Identify Barriers to Effective Communication and Improve Your Communication Skills

I0462859

By Meir Liraz

Published by BizMove

www.bizmove.com

ISBN: 9781090496812

Table of Contents

MEIR LIRAZ

1. Introduction

Most of us desire to communicate effectively, but do not have a keen appreciation of the barriers to be faced. Because of these barriers, there is ample opportunity for something to go wrong in any communication. Competent managers develop an awareness of the barriers and learn to cope with them.

How effectively do you, as a manager, communicate with your superiors, subordinates, and peers? Do you recognize the barriers to effective communication? Have you learned to cope with them? In the discussion that follows, the principal barriers to communicating effectively in today's working environment are identified, and proven techniques for coping with them are considered,

The principal barriers to effective communication are: noise, poor feedback, selection of inappropriate media, a wrong mental attitude, insufficient or lack of attention to work selection, delay in message transmittal, physical separation of the sender and receiver, and lack of empathy or a good relationship between the sender and receiver.

Let's examine each of these barriers and possible

steps to overcome them. As we conduct this examination, we should remember that any two or more of these barriers may occur in combination.

2. The Noise Barrier

Samuel Hoffenstein in his poem, "The Wind in the Trees," illustrates quite beautifully the distraction that noise may cause. He says:

When the wind is in the tree,

It makes a noise just like the sea,

As if there were not noise enough

To bother one, without that stuff.

Noise is any random or persistent disturbance that obscures, reduces, or confuses the clarity or quality of the message being transmitted. In other words, it is any interference that takes place between the sender and the receiver. This is why we generally identify any communication problem that can't be fully explained as "noise." The biggest single cause of noise in the communication process may be the assumption that the act of communicating is a simple process - that it doesn't require much thought or practice and all effective managers were born with this skill. This is not true. Effective communication comes with study and practice. The effectiveness of the communication process is dependent upon the capabilities of the senders and receivers.

To overcome the noise barrier to effective communication, one must discover its source. This may not be easy. Noise appears in a variety of ways. During a conversation, have you ever been distracted by the pictures on the wall, the view from the window, a report lying open on a desk, or a conversation taking place in an adjacent room? Many people have been so distracted.

In the perusal of a written communication, have you ever been confused by irrelevant material or the illogical approach taken by the author? Again, many people have.

Once the source, or sources, of the noise has been identified, steps can be taken to overcome it. The noise barrier can't always be overcome but, fortunately, just the awareness of its existence by either the sender or the receiver of a message can help to improve the communication flow.

3. The Feedback Problem

Feedback is reaction, Without it, the sender of the message cannot know whether the recipient has received the entire message or grasped its intent.

The need for feedback should be clearly understood. Feedback is the return of a portion of the message to the sender with new information. It regulates both the transmission and reception. The whole process is straightforward: the sender transmits the message via the most suitable communication media; the receiver gets the message, decodes it, and provides feedback.

In oral, face-to-face communication, the process doesn't happen quite this way. All of these actions occur almost simultaneously. For example, the sender is acting as a receiver while transmitting the message; the receiver is acting as a sender while receiving the message. When the message is transmitted and effectively received, feedback serves as a regulating device. The sender continually adjusts his transmission in response to the feedback. Feedback also alerts the sender to any disruptive noise that may impede reception of the message.

There is no feedback in a one-way communication.

Such a communication involves passing ideas, information, directions, and instructions from higher
management down the chain of command without
asking for a response or checking to see if any
action has taken place. It is not enough to ensure
the message has been received. For communication
to be effective, a two-way process must exist so the
sender knows whether the message has been
understood. The two-way communication process
involves sending a message down the chain of
command and transmitting a response containing
information, ideas, and feelings back up the chain.
This process has been referred to sometimes as "a
process of material influence."

Feedback not only regulates the communication
process, but reinforces and stimulates it. In fact, it
actually serves as the hallmark of dialogue, because
it forces communication and makes it dual. Dual
expression, when combined with mutual feedback,
becomes a dialogue.

4. The Problem of Media Selection

In any given situation the medium, or media, for communication must be selected. One medium may work better than another. However, in many cases a combination of media may be used for the communication process to function effectively.

Henry H. Albers says that no one communication medium can adequately serve the diverse functional and personal problems of organization dynamics. He believes that "a repetition of ideas in different terms is useful in solving some communication problems." The question then emerges, What combination of media would be most effective? Any project to develop the one best combination of media would prove rather fruitless. There are many combinations that can provide satisfactory results.

The personal qualities of the manager should be a consideration in media selection. As manager, you should recognize your strengths and limitations. You should evaluate your successes and failures in communication and plan to use the media that best fits your style and qualities.

Generally, managers make more frequent use of oral, rather than written, communication. However, the media one selects for communication in a particular situation should correlate with the feedback requirements. A communication failure or partial failure could occur if the media you select for transmittal of a message is inappropriate and necessary feedback is not received. Most simple messages can be transmitted orally - either in a face-to-face discussion, formal briefing, or meeting of the staff. More complex messages should be written in a directive, instruction, memorandum, or report. Very complex messages should be transmitted in both oral and written form. Repetition and review of an oral communication in written form can be a facilitating device.

5. The Mental Barrier

One principal barrier to effective communication is mental. It consists of noise in the mind of the sender or receiver. Here are four examples:

The arrogance of the sender may impair the communication process. If the sender believes he knows everything there is to know about the subject being transmitted, he expects acceptance of his ideas or directions. If the receiver disagrees with the sender and so states, the sender will not be attuned to the feedback or will find it a challenge to his stated position. Real communication does not take place.

The sender may assume the receiver will respond to his message in a logical and rational manner. The receiver's priorities, problems, or assumptions may differ from the sender's. The receiver's logic may even override that of the sender. In any of these instances, the sender might judge the receiver to be incompetent or even an obstructionist. Communication will fail.

The sender may assume he is completely logical and rational - that his position is right and must prevail. This assumption may be false and no communication takes place.

The sender may have some misconceptions, self-interests, or strong emotions about a particular idea or approach, of which he is not aware. However, these traits may be readily evident to the receiver, who may think the sender is hypocritical. This communication will fail, as may all future communications between this sender and receiver.

6. The Problem of Word Selection

We live in a "verbal" environment. Words constitute the most frequently used tool for communicating. Words usually facilitate communication; however, their careless, improper use in a given situation can create a communication barrier. Arthur Kudner, an advertising executive, once told his son: "All big things have little names such as life and death, peace and war, or dawn, day, night, hope, love, and home. Learn to use little words in a big way. It is hard to do, but they say what you mean. When you don't know what you mean - use big words; they often fool little people."

The words we use should be selected carefully. Dr. Rudolph Flesch, a specialist in words and communication, suggests a way to break through the word barrier:

Use familiar words in place of the unfamiliar

Use concrete words in place of the abstract

Use short words in place of long

Use single words in place of several

Unfortunately, almost every commonly used word

has more than one meaning. Also words have regional meanings or derive new meanings as a result of the development of new industries or fields. The meaning conveyed by the sender's words depends upon the experience and attitude of the receiver. Therefore, one way to penetrate the word barrier is for the sender to strive to speak or write in terms of the receiver's experience and attitude. The better able he is to do this, the more successful the communication will be. Dr. S. E. Hayakawa, a U.S. Senator from California, expressed it very well when he said, "The meanings of words are not in the words; they are in us."

7. The Time and Space Barriers

Both time and space (the physical separation between the sender and the receiver) may serve as barriers to effective communication.

You, as a manager, may often feel pressed by time constraints. You may feel there aren't enough hours to accomplish all tasks. One executive puts it this way, "If I can't get the work done in a 24-hour day, I have to work evenings." Caught in the network of your own problems, you may even assume that your subordinates know what you want them to do, and they will proceed to do it. Actually, this may not be the case. Because of your failure to communicate, you may not receive the end product you were expecting.

This same problem may occur when you geographically separate departments or functions of an organization. Quick eye-to-eye communication becomes difficult. The telephone may not provide the answer. The line may be busy when the call is placed, or the person being called may be out of the office.

Memoranda sometime provide the answer to the space barrier. However, this might turn out to be a one-way communication of directions or information. If the recipient of a memorandum doesn't understand the message, or if he mistakenly thinks he understands, the communication process fails.

8. Empathy and Other Relationships

Lack of empathy can create a barrier between the sender and receiver. Empathy, as defined in the Dictionary, is "understanding so intimate that the feelings, thoughts, and motives of one are readily comprehended by another." You can transmit a better message if you can put yourself in the receiver's place and analyze the message from his viewpoint. The same holds true for the receiver. He must be able to empathize with you. That is, the sender, as well as the receiver, must try to project himself into the other's personality if he wants' to increase his potential for effective communication.

The ability to empathize with someone else may not be easy. If you are to see things from another's viewpoint, you have to put aside your own prejudices and preconceptions. The receiver may be of a different race, creed, educational background, from a different section of the country, or have a different specialty or rank within the organization. Under these circumstances, the task of empathizing with the other member of the communication link is difficult. The task is further complicated if you believe that understanding another's viewpoint may pose a threat to your own.

To better communicate, we must try to see ourselves through the eyes of others in the communication link. By developing some empathy with the people to whom we will be directing messages, we might recognize the need to modify our messages from time to time before sending them.

Douglas McGregor, one of the leading authorities on management practices, has said: "It is a fairly safe generalization that difficulties in communication within an organization are more often than not, mere symptoms of underlying difficulties in relationships between parties involved. When communication is ineffective, one needs to look first at the nature of these relationships rather than at ways of improving communication".

The relationship between the people involved in any communication process may form a greater barrier to the effectiveness of the communication between them than any other barrier discussed here. If the relationship between the people participating in the communication is good, the communication has a greater chance for success. This is true whether the communication takes place in oral or written form.

The quality of the relationship between the sender and receiver determines to a great extent the ability of the person transmitting the message to penetrate the communication barrier.

Final Observations

We have examined the principal barriers to effective communication. We have seen all around us the problems resulting from the inability of people in today's working environment to penetrate these barriers. What are you going to do about it? Can you let the barriers to effective communication in your organization continue to block the path to effective management? If you and the persons with whom you communicate do your part to reduce these barriers, some of them may be eliminated. As a result, management of your organization will be enhanced. Why not take such action today?

MEIR LIRAZ

MEIR LIRAZ

www.ingramcontent.com/pod-product-compliance
Lightning Source LLC
Chambersburg PA
CBHW072311170526
45158CB00003BA/1281